# 40 HOURS

## AN ADORATION COMPANION

Foreword by Bishop Kevin C. Rhoades

WITH REFLECTIONS BY FR. JEFFREY KIRBY, STL

Our Sunday Visitor
Huntington, Indiana

*Nihil Obstat*
Msgr. Michael Heintz, Ph.D.
*Censor Librorum*

*Imprimatur*
✠ Kevin C. Rhoades
Bishop of Fort Wayne-South Bend
April 26, 2023

The *Nihil Obstat* and *Imprimatur* are official declarations that a book is free from doctrinal or moral error. It is not implied that those who have granted the Nihil Obstat and Imprimatur agree with the contents, opinions, or statements expressed.

Our Sunday Visitor Publishing Division, Our Sunday Visitor, Inc., 200 Noll Plaza, Huntington, IN 46750; www.osv.com;1-800-348-2440

ISBN: 978-1-68192-791-6 (Inventory No. T2787)
1. RELIGION—Christianity—Catholic.

eISBN: 978-1-63966-032-2
LCCN: 2023937611

Cover design: Tyler Ottinger
Cover art: Adobestock
Interior design: Amanda Falk

PRINTED IN THE UNITED STATES OF AMERICA

*Beloved brothers and sisters ... brother bishops, priests, deacons, men and women religious, all of you who see before you the infinite abasement of the Son of God and the infinite glory of the Resurrection, remain in silent adoration of your Lord, our Master and Lord Jesus Christ. Remain silent, then speak and tell the world: we cannot be silent about what we know. Go and tell the whole world the marvels of God, present at every moment of our lives, in every place on earth. May God bless us and keep us, may he lead us on the path of eternal life, he who is Life, for ever and ever. Amen.*

— Pope Benedict XVI, Meditation at Lourdes, 2008

•••

*It is beautiful to worship in silence before the Blessed Sacrament, to be in the consoling presence of Jesus and there to draw the apostolic impetus to be instruments of goodness, tenderness and welcome in the community, in the Church, and in the world.*

— Pope Francis, October 22, 2022

# Contents

# Foreword

Eucharistic devotion has been a part of my life ever since I can remember. As a young boy, I remember that whenever my family walked downtown (which was quite often), we would always stop in our parish church to make a visit to the Blessed Sacrament. We would kneel before the tabernacle and pray to Our Lord present there and often light a candle at the altar of our Blessed Mother. It was part of the regular rhythm of my life growing up.

I also recall the annual celebration of the Forty Hours Devotion as a highlight of parish life. Over a hundred people would be present at any given time during those forty hours praying before Jesus in the holy Eucharist. The church would be filled to overflowing for evening devotions during Forty Hours. The closing celebration on Tuesday evening would be attended by dozens of priests participating in the procession and included all of us who were altar boys. It was a joyful climax of the Forty Hours as together everyone sang the Eucharistic hymns by heart, voices united in expressing our heartfelt praise and thanksgiving for the awesome gift of the Body and Blood of the Lord, which we knew was our greatest treasure as Catholics.

The tradition of the Forty Hours Devotion remained strong in my home diocese for many years after my childhood. When I served as a priest, and then the bishop, of the diocese, the annual Forty Hours Devotion was still mandated for every parish of the diocese. I think the tradition remained strong because it was so deeply rooted there. The territory of the Diocese of Harrisburg had been part of the Diocese of Philadelphia when St. John Neumann was its bishop. Bishop Neumann had a great devotion to the holy Eucharist and was the first bishop in the United States to establish diocesan-wide Forty Hours devotions. Other bishops across the United States followed his lead when they heard about how the faithful flocked to adoration during Forty Hours in the Philadelphia diocese, bringing about a renewal of faith and devotion among the mostly immigrant Catholics in the United States at that time, a time in which anti-Catholic prejudice and bigotry was not uncommon.

The parish where I served as pastor in Harrisburg in the 1990s was the poorest of the diocese at the time and in a rough neighborhood of the city. The parish was appropriately under the patronage of St. Francis of Assisi. It was a multiethnic parish: majority Latino, with significant numbers of Black and older European American parishioners. During my pastorate, we also welcomed new Catholic immigrants from Vietnam. Our annual Forty Hours Devotion brought all our ethnic groups together to worship our Eucharistic Lord. I will never forget the closing liturgy as the community would sing praises of the Lord together in the different languages, with all the parish choirs, including the gospel choir leading the music. At the Forty Hours closing, we experienced that the Eucharist truly makes us "one body in Christ." Most, if not all, of the congregations in the neighborhood were separated by race or culture. It was beautiful to see our diverse Catholic congregation processing through the streets united in faith and love through our communion with Christ in the Eucharist. This public witness was an engine of evangelization in the neighborhood.

I am very happy and grateful that Our Sunday Visitor is publishing this book on the Forty Hours Devotion. We need such a concrete and practical guide for the revival of the devotion in our dioceses, one that updates the traditional Forty Hours liturgies according to the current liturgical norms and guidelines of the Church. With the impetus of the National Eucharistic Revival, we bishops are promoting greater devotion to the Blessed Sacrament. The revival of the Forty Hours Devotion is one way to promote it.

The liturgies and prayers in this book are helpful resources for both individual and communal prayer. Forty Hours is like a Eucharistic retreat in the midst of our busy lives. It is an opportunity for us to slow down a bit to spend time as a community of faith to focus our attention on the mystery of the holy Eucharist, to adore Jesus as truly Our Lord, present among us, to spend time with him in spiritual conversation; to pray for our families and friends, for our Church, our nation, and our world; and to receive from the Lord the strength, comfort, and support we need for our lives as his disciples.

When we worship the Eucharist outside of Mass, we enter into spiritual communion with the Lord whom we have received sacramentally in holy Communion. Prayer before Our Lord present in the holy Eucharist intensifies our friendship with him. It also helps us, in contemplating Our Lord's humility and love in the Eucharistic mystery, to live that mystery by allowing the graces we receive in holy Communion to bear more abundant fruit in our lives.

The Eucharist is the sacrament of Jesus' love for us unto the end. The Eucharistic sacrifice makes present the mystery of Our Lord's passion and death and also the mystery of his resurrection. The time frame of the Forty Hours Devotion reminds us of this truth since it recalls the forty hours between Christ's death and resurrection. The Eucharist teaches us and nourishes us to live the paschal mystery we celebrate, to love one another as he has loved us, and to grow in our life in Christ. The Eucharist is the food for the journey in our lives as disciples of Jesus Christ, the "new manna" for our journey to the promised land of heaven. We adore the new manna because it is "the living bread come down from heaven," the flesh and blood of the Incarnate Son of God.

May the revival of the Forty Hours Devotion contribute to a beautiful revival of faith and love for the holy Eucharist in the life of the Church in our nation, and a revival of faith and love in our lives as disciples of Jesus Christ, our crucified and risen Lord! May St. John Neumann intercede for us!

Bishop Kevin C. Rhoades
Diocese of Fort Wayne-South Bend

# I
# Overview

# 1

# What Is the Forty Hours Devotion?

*I am the bread of life; whoever comes to*
*me will never hunger, and whoever believes*
*in me will never thirst.* — John 6:35

The Forty Hours Devotion is a period of prayer for forty hours before the Lord truly present in the Blessed Sacrament. During this time, the holy Eucharist is solemnly exposed in a monstrance, a vessel that allows adorers to see the Sacred Host. Solemn exposition of the holy Eucharist for forty hours is based on the tradition that Christ's body remained in the tomb for forty hours after his burial until his resurrection.

Solemn exposition of the holy Eucharist for forty hours began as a liturgical devotion of the Church in Italy during the sixteenth century. Many great saints at the time of the Counter-Reformation advocated its practice, including Sts. Anthony Maria Zaccaria and Charles Borromeo in Milan, St. Philip Neri in Rome, and St. Ignatius Loyola and the early Jesuits throughout the mission fields of the Church. The holy Eucharist was at the heart of their evangelization and re-evangelization efforts. The popes at the time approved and encouraged the spread of the Forty Hours Devotion, including Pope Clement VIII, who wrote: "We have determined to establish publicly in this mother city of Rome an uninterrupted course of prayer in such ways that in the different churches, on appointed days, there be observed the pious and salutary devotion of the Forty Hours, with such an arrangement of churches and times that at every hour of the day and night, the whole year round, the incense of prayer shall ascend without intermission before the face of the Lord."

The Forty Hours Devotion spread throughout the world, including to the United States in the nineteenthth century. St. John Neumann, the fourth bishop of Philadelphia, had a deep devotion to the Lord present in the Blessed Sacrament and sought to bring the Forty Hours Devotion to his diocese. There was strong anti-Catholic sentiment in Philadelphia at that time — for example, two Catholic churches in the city were destroyed by arson — so there were fears that instituting Forty Hours in the city might inflame anti-Catholic activity, even profanation of the Blessed Sacrament. In prayer, Bishop Neumann heard the Lord telling him not to fear. He moved forward and mandated an annual Forty Hours Devotion in all the parishes of the diocese. The faithful participated with fervent piety. This success led to the spread of the Forty Hours Devotion to other dioceses. In 1866, at the Second Plenary Council of Baltimore, the U.S. bishops approved the Forty Hours Devotion for all dioceses of the United States.

The Church encourages the worship of the holy Eucharist outside Mass and the practice of an annual extended period of solemn exposition of the holy Eucharist, such as occurs with the traditional Forty Hours Devotion. The Roman Ritual *Holy Communion and Worship of the Eucharist Outside Mass* states: "In churches where the Eucharist is regularly reserved it is recommended that solemn exposition of the Blessed Sacrament for an extended period of time should take place once a year, even though this period is not strictly continuous. In this way the local community may reflect more profoundly upon this mystery and adore [Christ in the Sacrament]" (no. 86).

The Forty Hours Devotion need not last exactly forty hours.

Customarily in the United States, the forty hours extend across three days, often beginning at the end of a Sunday Mass and ending on Tuesday evening. The period of exposition is not strictly continuous since the holy Eucharist is reposed in the tabernacle during the time of Masses that are celebrated in the church during the forty hours. Ideally, this would be the only time that exposition would be interrupted; however, the Eucharist would need to be reposed if there is a time in which there would not be worshipers present.

Worship and adoration of the Lord present in the Blessed Sacrament during the Forty Hours Devotion draws individuals and the community into deeper intimacy with the Lord and his paschal mystery which becomes present in the Holy Sacrifice of the Mass. It is an opportunity to spend personal time with the Lord, to pour out our hearts to him, and to pray for our loved ones, for the Church, and for the world. It is an opportunity to give praise and thanks to the Lord for his redemptive love, to adore him in the sacrament of his love, and to grow in the grace we receive in holy Communion to bear witness to his love in the world.

In 2021, the bishops of the United States wrote: "We rejoice in the growing numbers of the faithful who pray in adoration before the Blessed Sacrament, a testament of faith in the Real Presence of the Lord in the Eucharist. We encourage this devotion, which helps all of us to be formed by the self-giving love we behold in the Lord's gift of himself in the Eucharist" (The Mystery of the Eucharist in the Life of the Church [no. 33]).

# 2

# The Celebration of the Forty Hours Devotion

The following liturgical notes incorporate the Church's current norms and guidelines for the Solemn Exposition of the Most Holy Eucharist.

## OPENING OF FORTY HOURS

The Forty Hours Devotion, held in a church or oratory where the holy Eucharist is reserved, begins at the end of the celebration of Mass, customarily at the last Mass on Sunday. At that Mass, the host to be used for adoration is consecrated. After the distribution of holy Communion, this Host is placed in the monstrance upon the altar where four to six candles are lighted. After the priest prays the Prayer after Communion, he proceeds to the front of the altar and incenses the Blessed Sacrament while *O Salutaris Hostia* (English translation: "O Victim Bringing Saving Grace") or another Eucharistic hymn is sung. The priest and liturgical ministers then depart. The usual concluding rites of the Mass (final blessing and dismissal) are omitted.

## PRAYER DURING THE FORTY HOURS

During the extended period of exposition of the most holy Eucharist (the Forty Hours), the faithful are encouraged to visit the church or oratory to pray before the Blessed Sacrament. There must always be adorers present and the exposed Blessed Sacrament may never be left unattended. Sacred silence is observed during most of the forty hours, allowing the faithful to enter into interior dialogue with the Lord in prayer, to meditate upon his word, to abide in his presence, and to adore him in the sacrament of his love.

During the Forty Hours Devotion, it is also important to worship the Lord through communal prayer. The Church recommends prayers, liturgical songs, and readings during Eucharistic exposition. The communal praying of Morning and Evening Prayer from the Liturgy of the Hours is especially recommended. In addition, or alternatively, the Liturgy of the Word may be celebrated during the Forty Hours. Homilies may be given during both these liturgies. In many places, it is customary to celebrate Forty Hours Devotion as a type of parish mission during which a priest or deacon preaches each evening on the mystery of the holy Eucharist. It is appropriate to have singing during these liturgies, including the chanting of the psalms.

Benediction with the Blessed Sacrament may be given at the end of the aforementioned liturgies. Before Benediction, while the priest or deacon is incensing the Blessed Sacrament, the *Tantum Ergo Sacramentum* (English translation: "Let Us, Therefore, Bow and Worship") or another Eucharistic hymn is sung. After Benediction, it is customary to pray the Divine Praises or another acclamation.

## SOLEMN CLOSING OF FORTY HOURS

If the Forty Hours Devotion began on Sunday, it typically ends on Tuesday evening with Evening Prayer or a Liturgy of the Word, with Benediction, as described above. It is also possible to close the Forty Hours with the celebration of Mass. In this case, Benediction is given and the Sacred Host is placed in the tabernacle before Mass begins.

The closing of the Forty Hours Devotion is celebrated with special solemnity. It is an opportunity for the whole parish to gather to give special thanks to the Lord for the great gift of his

Body and Blood in the holy Eucharist. It is helpful to offer catechesis to the faithful on worship of the Eucharist outside Mass in the weeks preceding the Forty Hours Devotion and to encourage their participation. The liturgies during Forty Hours should be carefully planned and include the participation of choir and musicians, especially for the closing celebration. It is customary to invite clergy and faithful from neighboring parishes to attend the closing celebration.*

---

*In the past, it was common to have a Eucharistic procession within the church or oratory during the closing of the Forty Hours Devotion. Eucharistic processions within the church or oratory are no longer permitted. They are to take place outside, as on the Solemnity of Corpus Christi. In such processions, the holy Eucharist in the monstrance is carried through the streets with songs and prayers as a public witness of faith and devotion to the Most Blessed Sacrament. With the bishop's approval, a Eucharistic procession may take place at the beginning or end of Forty Hours; however, it would need to be a procession through the streets and not merely within the church.

# II
# Public Devotions

# 3
# Exposition and Benediction

The monstrance is placed on the altar, and the host placed in the monstrance. The celebrant goes to the altar and incenses the holy eucharist. A suitable hymn — typically *O Salutaris Hostia*, given below — may be sung.

O Victim bringing saving grace,
who open wide the gate of heav'n:
our foes assail and press us hard;
give us your strength, bring us
    your aid.

O salutáris Hóstia,
quæ cæli pandis óstium,
bella premunt hostília:
da robur, fer auxílium.

To you be everlasting praise
and glory, One and Triune Lord,
who grant us life that knows
    no end,
for ever in our heav'nly home.
Amen.

Uni trinóque Dómino
sit sempitérna glória,
qui vitam sine término
nobis donet in pátria.
Amen.

The celebrant stands and sings or says:
Let us pray.

After a brief pause, he says a prayer:
O God, who in this wonderful Sacrament have left us a memorial of your Passion, grant us, we pray, so to revere the sacred mysteries of your Body and Blood that we may always experience in ourselves the fruits of your redemption. Who live and reign for ever and ever.

All respond:
**Amen.**

When the time of adoration has concluded, or is paused for Mass or a similar reason, the rite of Benediction follows.

The priest or deacon approaches the altar, genuflects and kneels, and the following or another hymn or other Eucharistic song is sung. Meanwhile the minister, while kneeling, incenses the Most Blessed Sacrament.

| | |
|---|---|
| **Let us, therefore, bow**<br>**and worship**<br>**such a wondrous Sacrament;**<br>**let the ancient law**<br>**and custom**<br>**to a newer rite now yield;**<br>**let our faith supply**<br>**conviction**<br>**where the senses tire and fail.** | **Tantum ergo Sacraméntum**<br>**venerémur cérnui,**<br>**et antíquum documéntum**<br>**novo cedat rítui;**<br>**præstet fides suppleméntum**<br>**sénsuum deféctui.** |
| **To the Father, unbegotten,**<br>**and the Sole-begotten Son,**<br>**be salvation, blessing, honor,**<br>**jubilation, power, and praise;**<br>**to the One from both**<br>**proceeding**<br>**equal glory and renown.**<br>**Amen.** | **Genitóri Genitóque**<br>**laus et iubilátio,**<br>**salus, honor, virtus quoque**<br>**sit et benedíctio;**<br>**procedénti ab utróque**<br>**compar sit laudátio. Amen.** |

Then the following verse and response may be added:

V. You have given them Bread from heaven (E.T. alleluia).
R. Having all sweetness within it (E.T. alleluia).

V. Panem de cælo præstitísti eis (T.P. allelúia).
R. Omne delectaméntum in se habéntem (T.P. allelúia).

The celebrant stands and sings or says:
Let us pray.

After a brief pause, he says a prayer.
O God, who in this wonderful Sacrament have left us a memorial of your Passion, grant us, we pray, so to revere the sacred mysteries of your Body and Blood that we may always experience in ourselves the fruits of your redemption. Who live and reign for ever and ever.

All respond:
Amen.

Alternative prayers may be found in *Holy Communion and Worship of the Eucharist Outside Mass*.

Once the prayer has been said, the Priest or Deacon puts on a humeral veil, genuflects, and then takes the monstrance or ciborium and, with it, makes the Sign of the Cross over the people, without saying anything. A minister may incense the Most Blessed Sacrament, if appropriate, as the Priest or Deacon makes the Sign of the Cross with it over the people.

In accordance with local custom, the following acclamations (the Divine Praises) may be sung or said in unison after the blessing with the Most Blessed Sacrament and before placing the Sacrament back in the tabernacle:

**Blessed be God.**
**Blessed be his holy Name.**
**Blessed be Jesus Christ, true God and true man.**
**Blessed be the Name of Jesus.**
**Blessed be his most Sacred Heart.**
**Blessed be his most Precious Blood.**
**Blessed be Jesus in the most holy Sacrament of the altar.**
**Blessed be the Holy Spirit, the Paraclete.**
**Blessed be the great Mother of God, Mary most holy.**
**Blessed be her holy and Immaculate Conception.**
**Blessed be her glorious Assumption.**
**Blessed be the name of Mary, Virgin and Mother.**
**Blessed be Saint Joseph, her most chaste Spouse.**
**Blessed be God in his Angels and in his Saints.**

He then removes the blessed sacrament from the monstrance and returns it to the tabernacle. At this time the people may sing an appropriate hymn while the ministers depart.

# 4

# Liturgy of the Hours
# Evening Prayer I

*After the people have assembled, the ministers approach the altar in silence or while instrumental music is played. If the blessed sacrament is already exposed, the ministers reverence it with a genuflection and go to their chairs. If the blessed sacrament is not exposed, the blessed sacrament is brought to the altar and placed in the monstrance. The presiding minister then goes to the altar, kneels, and incenses the holy eucharist. Meanwhile, a suitable song may be sung by the people, in which case the hymn below is omitted. After the incensation, the ministers go to their chairs.*

*Presider, making the sign of the cross:* **God, come to my assistance.**
     *All:* **Lord, make haste to help me.**
     Glory to the Father, and to the Son, and to the Holy Spirit: as it was in the beginning, is now, and will be forever. Amen. Alleluia. *(The alleluia is omitted during Lent.)*
     Pange Lingua *(Hail our Savior's Glorious Body) or another appropriate eucharistic hymn may be used (see Hymns).*
     *The antiphon is sung by the cantor, the choir, or the entire assembly before each psalm. The antiphon may be repeated by all at the end of the psalm or after each strophe. The alleluia at the end of an antiphon is omitted during Lent.*

## Antiphon 1
     The Lord is compassionate; he gives food to those who

fear him as a remembrance of his great deeds.

## Psalm 111

I will thank the Lord with all my heart
in the meeting of the just and their assembly.
Great are the works of the Lord;
to be pondered by all who love them.

Majestic and glorious his work,
his justice stands firm for ever.
He makes us remember his wonders.
The Lord is compassion and love.

He gives food to those who fear him;
keeps his covenant ever in mind.
He has shown his might to his people
by giving them the lands of the nations.

His works are justice and truth:
his precepts are all of them sure,
standing firm for ever and ever:
they are made in uprightness and truth.

He has sent deliverance to his people
and established his covenant for ever.
Holy his name, to be feared.

To fear the Lord is the beginning of wisdom;
all who do so prove themselves wise.
His praise shall last for ever!

Glory to the Father, and to the Son, and to the Holy Spirit:
— as it was in the beginning, is now, and will be for ever.

Amen.

*Ant.* The Lord is compassionate; he gives food to those
who fear him as a remembrance of his great deeds.

## Ant. 2
The Lord brings peace to his Church, and fills us with
the finest wheat.

## Psalm 147:12–20
O praise the Lord, Jerusalem!
Zion, praise your God!

He has strengthened the bars of your gates,
he has blessed the children within you.
He established peace on your borders,
he feeds you with finest wheat.

He sends out his word to the earth
and swiftly runs his command.
He showers down snow white as wool,
he scatters hoar-frost like ashes.

He hurls down hailstones like crumbs.
The waters are frozen at his touch;
he sends forth his word and it melts them:
at the breath of his mouth the waters flow.

He makes his word known to Jacob,
to Israel his laws and decrees.
He has not dealt thus with other nations;
he has not taught them his decrees.

Glory to the Father, and to the Son, and to the Holy Spirit:
— as it was in the beginning, is now, and will be for ever.
Amen.

*Ant.* The Lord brings peace to his Church, and fills us
with the finest wheat.

## Ant. 3

Truly I say to you: Moses did not give you the bread
from heaven; my Father gives you the true bread from
heaven, alleluia.

## Canticle — Revelation 11:17–18; 12:10b–12a

We praise you, the Lord God Almighty,
who is and who was.
You have assumed your great power,
you have begun your reign.

The nations have raged in anger,
but then came your day of wrath
and the moment to judge the dead:
The time to reward your servants the prophets
and the holy ones who revere you,
the great and the small alike.

Now have salvation and power come,
the reign of our God and the authority
of his Anointed One.
For the accuser of our brothers is cast out,
who night and day accused them before God.

They defeated him by the blood of the Lamb
and by the word of their testimony;

love for life did not deter them from death.
So rejoice, you heavens,
and you that dwell therein!

Glory to the Father, and to the Son, and to the Holy Spirit:
— as it was in the beginning, is now, and will be for ever.
Amen.

*Ant.* Truly I say to you: Moses did not give you the bread from heaven; my Father gives you the true bread from heaven, alleluia.

## READING

### 1 Corinthians 10:16–17

Is not the cup of blessing we bless a sharing in the blood of Christ? And is not the bread we break a sharing in the body of Christ? Because the loaf of bread is one, we, many though we are, are one body, for we all partake of the one loaf.

*A priest or deacon may give a brief homily, and a period of silence may be observed.*

## RESPONSORY

He gave them bread from heaven, alleluia, alleluia.
— He gave them bread from heaven, alleluia, alleluia.

Man has eaten the bread of angels,
— alleluia, alleluia.

Glory to the Father, and to the Son, and to the Holy Spirit,

— He gave them bread from heaven, alleluia, alleluia.

## CANTICLE OF MARY

### Antiphon

How kind and gentle you are, O Lord. You showed your goodness to your sons by giving them bread from heaven. You filled the hungry with good things, and the rich you sent away empty.

### Luke 1:46–55

My soul proclaims the greatness of the Lord,
my spirit rejoices in God my Savior
for he has looked with favor on his lowly servant.

From this day all generations will call me blessed:
the Almighty has done great things for me,
and holy is his Name.

He has mercy on those who fear him
in every generation.

He has shown the strength of his arm,
he has scattered the proud in their conceit.

He has cast down the mighty from their thrones,
and has lifted up the lowly.

He has filled the hungry with good things,
and the rich he has sent away empty.

He has come to the help of his servant Israel
for he has remembered his promise of mercy,

the promise he made to our fathers,
to Abraham and his children for ever.

Glory to the Father, and to the Son, and to the Holy Spirit:
— as it was in the beginning, is now, and will be for ever.
Amen.

*Ant.* How kind and gentle you are, O Lord. You showed
your goodness to your sons by giving them bread from
heaven. You filled the hungry with good things, and the
rich you sent away empty.

## INTERCESSIONS

Christ invites all to the supper in which he gives his
body and blood for the life of the world. Let us ask him:
*Christ, the bread of heaven, grant us everlasting life.*

Christ, Son of the living God, you commanded that this
thanksgiving meal be done in memory of you,
— enrich your Church through the faithful celebration
of these mysteries.
*Christ, the bread of heaven, grant us everlasting life.*

Christ, eternal priest of the Most High, you have commanded your priests to offer your sacraments,
— may they help them to exemplify in their lives the
meaning of the sacred mysteries which they celebrate.
*Christ, the bread of heaven, grant us everlasting life.*

Christ, bread from heaven, you form one body out of all
who partake of the one bread,
— refresh all who believe in you with harmony and
peace.

*Christ, the bread of heaven, grant us everlasting life.*

Christ, through your bread you offer the remedy for immortality and the pledge of future resurrection,
— restore health to the sick and living hope to sinners.
*Christ, the bread of heaven, grant us everlasting life.*

Christ, our king who is to come, you commanded that the mysteries which proclaim your death be celebrated until you return,
— grant that all who die in you may share in your resurrection.
*Christ, the bread of heaven, grant us everlasting life.*

Our Father
who art in heaven,
hallowed be thy name.
Thy kingdom come.
Thy will be done on earth,
as it is in heaven.
Give us this day our daily bread,
and forgive us our trespasses,
as we forgive those who trespass against us,
and lead us not into temptation,
but deliver us from evil.


## CONCLUDING PRAYER

O God,
who in this wonderful Sacrament
have left us a memorial of your Passion,
grant us, we pray, so to revere the sacred mysteries
of your Body and Blood that we may always experience

in ourselves the fruits of your redemption.
Who live and reign with God the Father in the unity of
the Holy Spirit,
God, for ever and ever.
— Amen.

# 5

# Liturgy of the Hours Morning Prayer

*A*fter the people have assembled, the ministers approach the altar in silence or while instrumental music is played. If the blessed sacrament is already exposed, the ministers reverence it with a genuflection and go to their chairs. If the blessed sacrament is not exposed, the blessed sacrament is brought to the altar and placed in the monstrance. The presiding minister then goes to the altar, kneels, and incenses the holy eucharist. Meanwhile, a suitable song may be sung by the people, in which case the hymn below is omitted. After the incensation, the ministers go to their chairs.

*Presider, making the sign of the cross:* **God, come to my assistance.**
     *All:* **Lord, make haste to help me.**

Glory to the Father, and to the Son, and to the Holy Spirit: as it was in the beginning, is now, and will be forever. Amen. Alleluia. *(The alleluia is omitted during Lent.)*

Pange Lingua *(Hail our Savior's Glorious Body) or another appropriate eucharistic hymn may be used (see Hymns).*

*The antiphon is sung by the cantor, the choir, or the entire assembly before each psalm. The antiphon may be repeated by all at the end of the psalm or after each strophe. The alleluia at the end of an antiphon is omitted during Lent.*

## Antiphon 1
You fed your people with the food of angels; you gave them bread from heaven, alleluia.

## Psalm 63:2–9

O God, you are my God, for you I long;
for you my soul is thirsting.
My body pines for you
like a dry, weary land without water.
So I gaze on you in the sanctuary
to see your strength and your glory.

For your love is better than life,
my lips will speak your praise.
So I will bless you all my life,
in your name I will lift up my hands.
My soul shall be filled as with a banquet,
my mouth shall praise you with joy.

On my bed I remember you.
On you I muse through the night
for you have been my help;
in the shadow of your wings I rejoice.
My soul clings to you;
your right hand holds me fast.

Glory to the Father, and to the Son, and to the Holy Spirit:
— as it was in the beginning, is now, and will be for ever.
Amen.

*Ant.* You fed your people with the food of angels; you
gave them bread from heaven, alleluia.

## Ant. 2

Holy priests will offer incense and bread to God, alleluia.

## Canticle — Daniel 3:57–88, 56

Bless the Lord, all you works of the Lord.
Praise and exalt him above all forever.
Angels of the Lord, bless the Lord.
You heavens, bless the Lord,
All you waters above the heavens, bless the Lord.
All you hosts of the Lord, bless the Lord.
Sun and moon, bless the Lord.
Stars of heaven, bless the Lord.

Every shower and dew, bless the Lord.
All you winds, bless the Lord.
Fire and heat, bless the Lord.
Cold and chill, bless the Lord.
Dew and rain, bless the Lord.
Frost and chill, bless the Lord.
Ice and snow, bless the Lord.
Nights and days, bless the Lord.
Light and darkness, bless the Lord.
Lightnings and clouds, bless the Lord.

Let the earth bless the Lord.
Praise and exalt him above all forever.
Mountains and hills, bless the Lord.
Everything growing from the earth, bless the Lord.
You springs, bless the Lord.
Seas and rivers, bless the Lord.
You dolphins and all water creatures, bless the Lord.
All you birds of the air, bless the Lord.
All you beasts, wild and tame, bless the Lord.
You sons of men, bless the Lord.

O Israel, bless the Lord.

Praise and exalt him above all forever.
Priests of the Lord, bless the Lord.
Servants of the Lord, bless the Lord.
Spirits and souls of the just, bless the Lord.
Holy men of humble heart, bless the Lord.
Hananiah, Azariah, Mishael, bless the Lord.
Praise and exalt him above all forever.

Let us bless the Father, and the Son, and the Holy Spirit.
Let us praise and exalt him above all for ever.
Blessed are you, Lord, in the firmament of heaven.
Praiseworthy and glorious and exalted above all for ever.

*Ant.* Holy priests will offer incense and bread to God, alleluia.

## Ant. 3

I will give to the one who is victorious the hidden bread
and a new name, alleluia.

## Psalm 149

Sing a new song to the Lord,
his praise in the assembly of the faithful.
Let Israel rejoice in its maker,
let Zion's sons exult in their king.
Let them praise his name with dancing
and make music with timbrel and harp.

For the Lord takes delight in his people.
He crowns the poor with salvation.
Let the faithful rejoice in their glory,
shout for joy and take their rest.
Let the praise of God be on their lips

and a two-edged sword in their hand,

to deal out vengeance to the nations
and punishment on all the peoples;
to bind their kings in chains
and their nobles in fetters of iron;
to carry out the sentence pre-ordained;
this honor is for all his faithful.

Glory to the Father, and to the Son, and to the Holy Spirit:
— as it was in the beginning, is now, and will be for ever.
Amen.

*Ant.* I will give to the one who is victorious the hidden
bread and a new name, alleluia.

## READING

### Malachi 1:11

From the rising of the sun, even to its setting,
my name is great among the nations;
And everywhere they bring sacrifice to my name,
and a pure offering;
For great is my name among the nations,
says the Lord of hosts.

*A priest or deacon may give a brief homily, and a period of silence
may be observed.*

## RESPONSORY

You bring forth bread from the earth, alleluia, alleluia.
— You bring forth bread from the earth, alleluia, alleluia.

And wine which gives warmth to men's hearts,
— alleluia, alleluia.

Glory to the Father, and to the Son, and to the Holy Spirit,
— You bring forth bread from the earth, alleluia, alleluia.

## CANTICLE OF ZECHARIAH

### Antiphon
I am the living bread come down from heaven; anyone who eats this bread will live for ever, alleluia.

### Luke 1:68–79
Blessed be the Lord, the God of Israel;
he has come to his people and set them free.
He has raised up for us a mighty savior,
born of the house of his servant David.

Through his holy prophets he promised of old
that he would save us from our enemies,
from the hands of all who hate us.
He promised to show mercy to our fathers
and to remember his holy covenant.

This was the oath he swore to our father Abraham:
to set us free from the hands of our enemies,
free to worship him without fear,
holy and righteous in his sight all the days of our life.

You, my child, shall be called the prophet of the Most
    High;
for you will go before the Lord to prepare his way,
to give his people knowledge of salvation

by the forgiveness of their sins.

In the tender compassion of our God
the dawn from on high shall break upon us,
to shine on those who dwell in darkness and the shadow of death,
and to guide our feet into the way of peace.

Glory to the Father, and to the Son, and to the Holy Spirit:
— as it was in the beginning, is now, and will be for ever.
Amen.

*Ant.* I am the living bread come down from heaven; anyone who eats this bread will live for ever, alleluia.

## INTERCESSIONS

Brethren, let us pray to Jesus Christ, the bread of life, as we joyfully say:
*Happy are those who are called to your heavenly banquet.*

Priest of the new and eternal covenant, you offered perfect sacrifice to the Father on the altar of the cross,
— teach us to offer ourselves with you.
*Happy are those who are called to your heavenly banquet.*

King of justice and peace, you consecrated bread and wine as the sign of your offering,
— unite us as victims with you.
*Happy are those who are called to your heavenly banquet.*

True worshiper of the Father, your perfect offering is celebrated by the Church from the rising to the setting of the sun,

— unite in your body those who partake of the one bread.
*Happy are those who are called to your heavenly banquet.*

Manna from heaven, you nourish the Church with your body and blood,
— grant that we may walk strengthened by this food.
*Happy are those who are called to your heavenly banquet.*

Unseen host of our banquet, you stand at the door and knock,
— come to us, stay and share the evening meal with us.
*Happy are those who are called to your heavenly banquet.*

Our Father
who art in heaven,
hallowed be thy name.
Thy kingdom come.
Thy will be done on earth,
as it is in heaven.
Give us this day our daily bread,
and forgive us our trespasses,
as we forgive those who trespass against us,
and lead us not into temptation,
but deliver us from evil.

## CONCLUDING PRAYER

O God,
who in this wonderful Sacrament
have left us a memorial of your Passion,
grant us, we pray, so to revere the sacred mysteries
of your Body and Blood that we may always experience
in ourselves the fruits of your redemption.
Who live and reign with God the Father in the unity of

the Holy Spirit,
God, for ever and ever.
— Amen.

# 6
# Liturgy of the Hours
# Evening Prayer II

*A*fter the people have assembled, the ministers approach the altar in silence or while instrumental music is played. If the blessed sacrament is already exposed, the ministers reverence it with a genuflection and go to their chairs. If the blessed sacrament is not exposed, the blessed sacrament is brought to the altar and placed in the monstrance. The presiding minister then goes to the altar, kneels, and incenses the holy eucharist. Meanwhile, a suitable song may be sung by the people, in which case the hymn below is omitted. After the incensation, the ministers go to their chairs.

*Presider, making the sign of the cross:* **God, come to my assistance.**
 *All:* **Lord, make haste to help me.**

Glory to the Father, and to the Son, and to the Holy Spirit: as it was in the beginning, is now, and will be forever. Amen. Alleluia. *(The alleluia is omitted during Lent.)*

Pange Lingua *(Hail our Savior's Glorious Body) or another appropriate eucharistic hymn may be used (see Hymns).*

*The antiphon is sung by the cantor, the choir, or the entire assembly before each psalm. The antiphon may be repeated by all at the end of the psalm or after each strophe. The alleluia at the end of an antiphon is omitted during Lent.*

## Antiphon 1
Christ the Lord is a priest for ever in the line of Melchizedek; he offered up bread and wine.

## Psalm 110:1–5, 7

The Lord's revelation to my Master:
"Sit on my right:
your foes I will put beneath your feet."

The Lord will wield from Zion
your scepter of power:
rule in the midst of all your foes.

A prince from the day of your birth
on the holy mountains;
from the womb before the dawn I begot you.

The Lord has sworn an oath he will not change.
"You are a priest for ever,
a priest like Melchizedeck of old."

The Master standing at your right hand
will shatter kings in the day of his wrath.

He shall drink from the stream by the wayside
and therefore he shall lift up his head.

Glory to the Father, and to the Son, and to the Holy Spirit:
— as it was in the beginning, is now, and will be for ever.
Amen.

*Ant.* Christ the Lord is a priest for ever in the line of Melchizedek; he offered up bread and wine.

## Ant. 2

I will take up the cup of salvation, and I will offer a sacrifice of praise.

## Psalm 116:10–19

I trusted, even when I said:
"I am sorely afflicted,"
and when I said in my alarm:
"No man can be trusted."

How can I repay the Lord
for his goodness to me?
The cup of salvation I will raise;
I will call on the Lord's name.

My vows to the Lord I will fulfill
before all his people.
O precious in the eyes of the Lord
is the death of his faithful.

Your servant, Lord, your servant am I;
you have loosened my bonds.
A thanksgiving sacrifice I make:
I will call on the Lord's name.

My vows to the Lord I will fulfill
before all his people,
in the courts of the house of the Lord,
in your midst, O Jerusalem.

Glory to the Father, and to the Son, and to the Holy
Spirit:
— as it was in the beginning, is now, and will be for
ever. Amen.

*Ant.* I will take up the cup of salvation, and I will offer a
sacrifice of praise.

## Ant. 3

You are the way, the truth and the life of the world, O Lord.

## Canticle – see Revelation 19:1–7

Alleluia.
Salvation, glory, and power to our God:
his judgments are honest and true.
— Alleluia.

Alleluia.
Sing praise to our God, all you his servants,
all who worship him reverently, great and small.
— Alleluia.

Alleluia.
The Lord our all-powerful God is King;
Let us rejoice, sing praise, and give him glory.
— Alleluia.

Alleluia.
The wedding feast of the Lamb has begun,
and his bride is prepared to welcome him.
— Alleluia.

Glory to the Father, and to the Son, and to the Holy
Spirit:
— as it was in the beginning, is now, and will be for
ever. Amen.

*Ant.* You are the way, the truth and the life of the world,
O Lord.

# READING — 1 CORINTHIANS 11:23–25

I received from the Lord what I handed on to you, namely, that the Lord Jesus on the night in which he was betrayed took bread, and after he had given thanks, broke it and said, "This is my body, which is for you. Do this in remembrance of me." In the same way, after the supper, he took the cup, saying, "This cup is the new covenant in my blood. Do this, whenever you drink it, in remembrance of me."

*A priest or deacon may give a brief homily, and a period of silence may be observed.*

## RESPONSORY

He gave them bread from heaven, alleluia, alleluia.
— He gave them bread from heaven, alleluia, alleluia.

Man has eaten the bread of angels,
— alleluia, alleluia.

Glory to the Father, and to the Son, and to the Holy Spirit,
— He gave them bread from heaven, alleluia, alleluia.

## CANTICLE OF MARY

### Antiphon

How holy this feast in which Christ is our food; his passion is recalled; grace fills our hearts; and we receive a pledge of the glory to come, alleluia.

## Luke 1:46–55

My soul proclaims the greatness of the Lord,
my spirit rejoices in God my Savior
for he has looked with favor on his lowly servant.

From this day all generations will call me blessed:
the Almighty has done great things for me,
and holy is his Name.

He has mercy on those who fear him
in every generation.

He has shown the strength of his arm,
he has scattered the proud in their conceit.

He has cast down the mighty from their thrones,
and has lifted up the lowly.

He has filled the hungry with good things,
and the rich he has sent away empty.

He has come to the help of his servant Israel
for he has remembered his promise of mercy,
the promise he made to our fathers,
to Abraham and his children for ever.

Glory to the Father, and to the Son, and to the Holy Spirit:
— as it was in the beginning, is now, and will be for ever. Amen.

*Ant.* How holy this feast in which Christ is our food; his passion is recalled; grace fills our hearts; and we receive a pledge of the glory to come, alleluia.

## INTERCESSIONS

Christ invites all to the supper in which he gives his body and blood for the life of the world. Let us ask him:
*Christ, the bread of heaven, grant us everlasting life.*

Christ, Son of the living God, you commanded that this thanksgiving meal be done in memory of you,
— enrich your Church through the faithful celebration of these mysteries.
*Christ, the bread of heaven, grant us everlasting life.*

Christ, eternal priest of the Most High, you have commanded your priests to offer your sacraments,
— may they help them to exemplify in their lives the meaning of the sacred mysteries which they celebrate.
*Christ, the bread of heaven, grant us everlasting life.*

Christ, bread from heaven, you form one body out of all who partake of the one bread,
— refresh all who believe in you with harmony and peace.
*Christ, the bread of heaven, grant us everlasting life.*

Christ, through your bread you offer the remedy for immortality and the pledge of future resurrection,
— restore health to the sick and living hope to sinners.
*Christ, the bread of heaven, grant us everlasting life.*

Christ, our king who is to come, you commanded that the mysteries which proclaim your death be celebrated until you return,

— grant that all who die in you may share in your resurrection.
*Christ, the bread of heaven, grant us everlasting life.*

## CONCLUDING PRAYER
O God,
who in this wonderful Sacrament
have left us a memorial of your Passion,
grant us, we pray, so to revere the sacred mysteries
of your Body and Blood that we may always experience
in ourselves the fruits of your redemption.
Who live and reign with God the Father in the unity of
the Holy Spirit,
God, for ever and ever.
— Amen.

# 7

# Liturgy of the Word Prayer Service

The service given here is meant as an example or model; it may be adapted with alternative hymns, readings, prayers, intercessions, etc.

**Processional Hymn:** Lord, Who at Thy First Eucharist Did Pray

> Lord, who at thy first Eucharist did pray
> That all thy Church might be forever one,
> Grant us at ev'ry Eucharist to say
> With longing heart and soul, "Thy will be done."
> O may we all one bread, one body be,
> Through this blest Sacrament of Unity.
>
> At that first Eucharist before you died,
> O Lord, you prayed that all be one in you;
> At this our Eucharist again preside,
> And in our hearts your law of love renew.
> O may we all one bread, one body be,
> Through this blest Sacrament of Unity.
>
> For all thy Church, O Lord, we intercede;
> Make thou our sad divisions soon to cease;
> Draw us the nearer each, to each we plead,
> By drawing all to thee, O Prince of Peace;
> Thus may we all one bread, one body be,

Through this blest Sacrament of Unity.

We pray thee, too, for wand'rers from thy fold;
O bring them back, Good Shepherd of the sheep,
Back to the faith which saints believed of old,
Back to the Church which still that faith doth keep;
Soon may we all one bread, one body be,
Through this blest Sacrament of Unity.

So, Lord, at length when sacraments shall cease,
May we be one with all thy Church above,
One with thy saints in one unbroken peace,
One with thy saints in one unbounded love;
More blessed still in peace and love to be
One with the Trinity in Unity.

*If the blessed sacrament is not already exposed, the minister continues with exposition.*

*After a period of silent adoration, the liturgy of the word continues. A suitable pause for silent reflection should follow each reading.*

*Lector*: **A reading from the book of Exodus.**

## FIRST READING: EXODUS 16:2–4, 12–15

The whole Israelite community grumbled against Moses and Aaron.
The Israelites said to them,
"Would that we had died at the LORD's hand in the land of Egypt,
as we sat by our fleshpots and ate our fill of bread!
But you had to lead us into this desert
to make the whole community die of famine!"

Then the LORD said to Moses,
"I will now rain down bread from heaven for you.
Each day the people are to go out and gather their daily
     portion;
thus will I test them,
to see whether they follow my instructions or not.

"I have heard the grumbling of the Israelites.
Tell them: In the evening twilight you shall eat flesh,
and in the morning you shall have your fill of bread,
so that you may know that I, the LORD, am your God."

In the evening quail came up and covered the camp.
In the morning a dew lay all about the camp,
and when the dew evaporated, there on the surface of
     the desert
were fine flakes like hoarfrost on the ground.
On seeing it, the Israelites asked one another, "What is
     this?"
for they did not know what it was.
But Moses told them,
"This is the bread that the LORD has given you to eat."

*Lector*: **The Word of the Lord**
*All*: Thanks be to God.

## RESPONSORIAL PSALM:
## PSALM 34:2–3, 4–5, 6–7, 8–9

R. (9a) **Taste and see the goodness of the Lord.**

I will bless the LORD at all times;
his praise shall be ever in my mouth.

Let my soul glory in the LORD;
the lowly will hear me and be glad.

R. **Taste and see the goodness of the Lord.**

Glorify the LORD with me,
Let us together extol his name.
I sought the LORD, and he answered me
And delivered me from all my fears.

R. **Taste and see the goodness of the Lord.**

Look to him that you may be radiant with joy.
And your faces may not blush with shame.
When the afflicted man called out, the LORD heard,
And from all his distress he saved him.

R. **Taste and see the goodness of the Lord.**

The angel of the LORD encamps
around those who fear him and delivers them.
Taste and see how good the LORD is;
blessed the man who takes refuge in him.

R. **Taste and see the goodness of the Lord.**

*Priest or deacon:* **The Lord be with you.**
*All:* **And with your spirit.**
*Priest:* **A reading from the holy gospel according to John.**
*All:* **Glory to you, O Lord.**

## GOSPEL: JOHN 6:47-58

Amen, amen, I say to you, whoever believes has eternal life.

I am the bread of life.

Your ancestors ate the manna in the desert, but they died;

this is the bread that comes down from heaven so that one may eat it and not die.

I am the living bread that came down from heaven; whoever eats this bread will live forever; and the bread that I will give is my flesh for the life of the world."

The Jews quarreled among themselves, saying, "How can this man give us [his] flesh to eat?"

Jesus said to them, "Amen, amen, I say to you, unless you eat the flesh of the Son of Man and drink his blood, you do not have life within you.

Whoever eats my flesh and drinks my blood has eternal life, and I will raise him on the last day.

For my flesh is true food, and my blood is true drink.

Whoever eats my flesh and drinks my blood remains in me and I in him.

Just as the living Father sent me and I have life because of the Father, so also the one who feeds on me will have life because of me.

This is the bread that came down from heaven. Unlike your ancestors who ate and still died, whoever eats this bread will live forever."

*Priest or deacon:* **The gospel of the Lord.**
*All:* **Praise to you, Lord Jesus Christ.**

## HOMILY OR READING FROM
## THE CHURCH FATHERS

*At the conclusion of the last reading a priest or deacon may give a homily from the Scripture passages proclaimed. There may be a period of silent reflection after the homily. In place of the homily, a reading from one of the Church Fathers may be selected, such as the following:*

### From a work by Saint Thomas Aquinas, priest

Since it was the will of God's only begotten Son that men should share in his divinity, he assumed our nature in order that by becoming man he might make men gods. Moreover, when he took our flesh he dedicated the whole of its substance to our salvation. He offered his body to God the Father on the altar of the cross as a sacrifice for our reconciliation.

He shed his blood for our ransom and purification, so that we might be redeemed from our wretched state of bondage and cleansed from all sin.

But to ensure that the memory of so great a gift would abide with us for ever, he left his body as food and his blood as drink for the faithful to consume in the form of bread and wine.

O precious and wonderful banquet, that brings us salvation and contains all sweetness! Could anything be of more intrinsic value? Under the old law it was the flesh of calves and goats that was offered, but here Christ himself, the true God, is set before us as our food. What could be more wonderful than this? No other sacrament has greater healing power; through it sins are purged away, virtues are increased, and the soul is enriched with an abundance of every spiritual gift.

It is offered in the Church for the living and the

dead, so that what was instituted for the salvation of all may be for the benefit of all. Yet, in the end, no one can fully express the sweetness of this sacrament, in which spiritual delight is tasted at its very source, and in which we renew the memory of that surpassing love for us which Christ revealed in his passion.

It was to impress the vastness of this love more firmly upon the hearts of the faithful that our Lord instituted this sacrament at the Last Supper. As he was on the point of leaving the world to go to the Father, after celebrating the Passover with his disciples, he left it as a perpetual memorial of his passion.

It was the fulfillment of ancient figures and the greatest of all his miracles, while for those who were to experience the sorrow of his departure, it was destined to be a unique and abiding consolation.

## INTERCESSIONS

Christ invites all to the supper in which he gives his body and blood for the life of the world. Let us ask him:
*Christ, the bread of heaven, grant us everlasting life.*

Christ, Son of the living God, you commanded that this thanksgiving meal be done in memory of you; enrich your Church through the faithful celebration of these mysteries.
*Christ, the bread of heaven, grant us everlasting life.*

Christ, eternal priest of the Most High, you have commanded your priests to offer your sacraments; may they help them to exemplify in their lives the meaning of the sacred mysteries which they celebrate.
*Christ, the bread of heaven, grant us everlasting life.*

Christ, bread from heaven, you form one body out of all who partake of the one bread; refresh all who believe in you with harmony and peace.
*Christ, the bread of heaven, grant us everlasting life.*

Christ, through your bread you offer the remedy for immortality and the pledge of future resurrection; restore health to the sick and living hope to sinners.
*Christ, the bread of heaven, grant us everlasting life.*

Christ, our king who is to come, you commanded that the mysteries which proclaim your death be celebrated until you return; grant that all who die in you may share in your resurrection.
*Christ, the bread of heaven, grant us everlasting life.*

# III
# Public and Private Prayers

# 8
# Litanies

## LITANY OF THE HOLY EUCHARIST

| | |
|---|---|
| Lord, have mercy | **Lord, have mercy.** |
| Christ, have mercy | **Christ, have mercy.** |
| Lord, have mercy | **Lord, have mercy.** |
| Jesus, the Most High | **have mercy on us.** |
| Jesus, the holy One | **have mercy on us.** |
| Jesus, Word of God | **have mercy on us.** |
| Jesus, only Son of the Father | **have mercy on us.** |
| Jesus, Son of Mary | **have mercy on us.** |
| Jesus, crucified for us | **have mercy on us.** |
| Jesus, risen from the dead | **have mercy on us.** |
| Jesus, reigning in glory | **have mercy on us.** |
| Jesus, coming in glory | **have mercy on us.** |
| Jesus, our Lord | **have mercy on us.** |
| Jesus, our hope | **have mercy on us.** |
| Jesus, our peace | **have mercy on us.** |
| Jesus, our Savior | **have mercy on us.** |
| Jesus, our salvation | **have mercy on us.** |
| Jesus, our resurrection | **have mercy on us.** |
| Jesus, Judge of all | **have mercy on us.** |
| Jesus, Lord of the Church | **have mercy on us.** |
| Jesus, Lord of creation | **have mercy on us.** |
| Jesus, Lover of all | **have mercy on us.** |
| Jesus, life of the world | **have mercy on us.** |
| Jesus, freedom for<br>the imprisoned | **have mercy on us.** |

| | |
|---|---|
| Jesus, joy of the sorrowing | **have mercy on us.** |
| Jesus, giver of the Spirit | **have mercy on us.** |
| Jesus, giver of good gifts | **have mercy on us.** |
| Jesus, source of new life | **have mercy on us.** |
| Jesus, Lord of life | **have mercy on us.** |
| Jesus, eternal high priest | **have mercy on us.** |
| Jesus, priest and victim | **have mercy on us.** |
| Jesus, true Shepherd | **have mercy on us.** |
| Jesus, true Light | **have mercy on us.** |
| Jesus, bread of heaven | **have mercy on us.** |
| Jesus, bread of life | **have mercy on us.** |
| Jesus, bread of thanksgiving | **have mercy on us.** |
| Jesus, life-giving bread | **have mercy on us.** |
| Jesus, holy manna | **have mercy on us.** |
| Jesus, new covenant | **have mercy on us.** |
| Jesus, food for everlasting life | **have mercy on us.** |
| Jesus, food for our journey | **have mercy on us.** |
| Jesus, holy banquet | **have mercy on us.** |
| Jesus, true sacrifice | **have mercy on us.** |
| Jesus, perfect sacrifice | **have mercy on us.** |
| Jesus, eternal sacrifice | **have mercy on us.** |
| Jesus, divine Victim | **have mercy on us.** |
| Jesus, Mediator of the new covenant | **have mercy on us.** |
| Jesus, mystery of the altar | **have mercy on us.** |
| Jesus, medicine of immortality | **have mercy on us.** |
| Jesus, pledge of eternal glory | **have mercy on us.** |
| Jesus, Lamb of God, you take away the sins of the world | **have mercy on us.** |
| Jesus, Bearer of our sins, you take away the sins of the world | **have mercy on us.** |

| | |
|---|---|
| Jesus, Redeemer of the world, you take away the sins of the world | **have mercy on us.** |
| Christ, hear us | **Christ, hear us.** |
| Christ, graciously hear us | **Christ, graciously hear us.** |
| Lord Jesus, hear our prayer | **Lord Jesus, hear our prayer.** |

## LITANY FOR SOLEMN INTERCESSIONS

In those sections which contain several sets of invocations marked by A and B, one or the other may be chosen as desired. Some petitions adapted to local circumstances may be added to the petitions for various needs.

### I. Prayer to God

**A.**

| | |
|---|---|
| Lord, have mercy. | **Lord, have mercy.** |
| Christ, have mercy. | **Christ, have mercy.** |
| Lord, have mercy. | **Lord, have mercy.** |

**B.**

| | |
|---|---|
| God our Father in Heaven, | **have mercy on us.** |
| God the Son, Redeemer of the world, | **have mercy on us.** |
| God the Holy Spirit, | **have mercy on us.** |
| Holy Trinity, one God, | **have mercy on us.** |

### II. Invocation of Christ

**A.**

| | |
|---|---|
| Lord, be merciful, | **Lord, save your people.** |
| From all evil, | **Lord, save your people.** |
| From every sin, | **Lord, save your people.** |

| | |
|---|---|
| From anger and hatred, | **Lord, save your people.** |
| From every evil intention, | **Lord, save your people.** |
| From everlasting death, | **Lord, save your people.** |
| By your coming as man, | **Lord, save your people.** |
| By your birth | **Lord, save your people.** |
| By your baptism and holy fasting, | **Lord, save your people.** |
| By your sufferings and cross, | **Lord, save your people.** |
| By your death and burial, | **Lord, save your people.** |
| By your rising to new life, | **Lord, save your people.** |
| By your return in glory to the Father, | **Lord, save your people.** |
| By your gift of the Holy Spirit, | **Lord, save your people.** |
| By your coming again in glory, | **Lord, save your people.** |

**B.**

| | |
|---|---|
| Christ, Son of the living God, | **have mercy on us.** |
| You came into this world, | **have mercy on us.** |
| You suffered for us on the cross | **have mercy on us.** |
| You died to save us, | **have mercy on us.** |
| You lay in the tomb, | **have mercy on us.** |
| You rose from the dead, | **have mercy on us.** |
| You returned in glory to the Father, | **have mercy on us.** |
| You sent the Holy Spirit upon your Apostles, | **have mercy on us.** |
| You are seated at the right hand of the Father, | **have mercy on us.** |
| You will come again to judge the living and the dead, | **have mercy on us.** |

### III. *Prayer for Various Needs*
**A.**

| | |
|---|---|
| Lord, be merciful to us, | **Lord, hear our prayer.** |
| Give us true repentance, | **Lord, hear our prayer.** |
| Strengthen us in your service, | **Lord, hear our prayer.** |
| Reward with eternal life all who do good to us, | **Lord, hear our prayer.** |
| Bless the fruits of the earth and of our labor, | **Lord, hear our prayer.** |

**B.**

| | |
|---|---|
| Lord, show us your kindness, | **Lord, hear our prayer.** |
| Raise our thoughts and desires to you, | **Lord, hear our prayer.** |
| Grant eternal rest to all who have died in the faith, | **Lord, hear our prayer.** |
| Spare us from disease, hunger, and war, | **Lord, hear our prayer.** |
| Bring all peoples together in trust and peace. | **Lord, hear our prayer.** |

The following section is always used.

| | |
|---|---|
| Guide and protect your holy Church, | **Lord, hear our prayer.** |
| Keep the pope and all the clergy in faithful service to your Church, | **Lord, hear our prayer.** |
| Bring all Christians together in unity, | **Lord, hear our prayer.** |
| Lead all to the light of the Gospel, | **Lord, hear our prayer.** |

## IV. Conclusion
### A.

Christal Christ, hear us,          **Christ, graciously
                                     hear us.**

Lord Jesus, hear our prayer       **Lord Jesus, hear our
                                     prayer.**

### B.

Lamb of God, who takes away
   the sins of the world,          **spare us, O Lord!**
Lamb of God, who takes away
   the sins of the world,          **graciously hear us, O
                                     Lord!**

Lamb of God, who takes away
   the sins of the world,          **Have mercy on us.**

# 9
# Suggested Hymns

*Adoro Te Devote*/Humbly We Adore Thee
Alleluia! Sing to Jesus
Be Thou My Vision
Bread of the World, in Mercy Broken
Christ Be Beside Me/St. Patrick's Breastplate
Come, My Way, My Truth, My Life
*Creator Alme Siderum*/Creator of the Stars of Night
Day is Done, But Love Unfailing
Father, We Thank Thee Who Hast Planted
Holy God, We Praise Thy Name
Immortal, Invisible, God Only Wise
Jesus, My Lord, My God, My All
Let All Mortal Flesh Keep Silence
Lord of All Hopefulness
Lord Who At Thy First Eucharist Did Pray
O Jesus, We Adore Thee
O Radiant Light
*O Salutaris Hostia*/O Saving Victim
*Pange Lingua*/Hail Our Savior's Glorious Body
*Panis Angelicus*
Sing, My Tongue, the Savior's Glory
Soul of My Savior
*Tantum Ergo*
The King of Love My Shepherd Is
*Ubi Caritas*/Where Charity and Love Prevail

# 10
# Prayers

## PRAYERS FROM THE OPENING RITES OF THE 40 HOURS DEVOTION, 1950[*]

V. Preserve your servants
R. Who trust in you, my God.

V. Be for us, O Lord, a tower of strength,
R. In the face of the enemy.

V. Let the enemy do nothing to harm us,
R. And the son of iniquity have no power over us.

V. O Lord, deal not with us according to our sins,
R. Nor take retribution on us because of our transgressions.

V. Let us pray for our Sovereign Pontiff, [Name]
R. The Lord preserve him, and give him life, and make him blessed upon the earth, and not deliver him up to the will of his enemies.

V. Let us pray for our benefactors,
R. For your name's sake, O Lord, reward with eternal life all those who do us good. Amen.

---

*The Reverend Philip T. Weller, trans. & ed., *The Roman Ritual: Volume I, The Sacraments and Processions,* (Milwaukee: The Bruce Publishing Company, 1950), 289-293.

V. Let us pray for the faithful departed.
R. Eternal rest grant unto them, O Lord, and let perpetual light shine upon them.

V. May they rest in peace.
R. Amen.

V. For our absent brethren.
R. Preserve your servants who trust in you, O my God.

V. Send them, Lord, aid from on high.
R. And from Sion watch over them.

V. O Lord, hear my prayer.
R. And let my cry come unto you.

V. The Lord be with you.
R. And with your spirit.

Let us pray.
O God, who in this wonderful Sacrament have left us a memorial of your Passion, grant us, we pray, so to revere the sacred mysteries of your Body and Blood that we may always experience in ourselves the fruits of your redemption.

Almighty, everlasting God, have mercy on your servant, N., our Sovereign Pontiff, and direct him according to your clemency on the way to eternal salvation, that by your grace he may both desire the things that please you, and strive with his whole might to execute them.

O God, our refuge and our strength, give ear to the entreaties of your Church, o Source of mercy, and grant that what we seek with faith, we may receive in fact.

Almighty, everlasting God, Who has dominion over the living and the dead, and are merciful to all whom you foreknow shall be your by faith and good works; we, your suppliants pray, that those for whom we pour forth our petitions, whether this present world still detain them in the flesh, or the world to come has already received their souls, may by your benign goodness and through the intercession of your saints, obtain pardon for all their sins. Through our Lord, Jesus Christ, your Son, Who lives and reigns with you in the unity of the Holy Spirit, God, forever and ever.

Amen.

V. O Lord, hear my prayer.
R. And let my cry come unto you.

V. May the almighty and merciful Lord graciously hear us.
R. And may he watch over us at all times. Amen.

V. May the souls of the faithful departed, through the mercy of God, rest in peace.
R. Amen.

## PRAYER OF REPARATION TO THE EUCHARISTIC HEART OF JESUS

May the Heart of Jesus in the most Blessed Sacrament be praised, adored, and loved with grateful affection at every moment in all the tabernacles of the world, now and until the end of time. Amen.

## A PRAYER FOR GREATER DEVOTION TO OUR LORD IN THE BLESSED SACRAMENT*

I beseech you, O Lord, to have compassion upon me, and to inflame my heart with ardent love and zeal for your honor and glory; make me through your grace always so to believe and understand, to feel and firmly hold, to speak and think of the exceeding mystery of this Blessed Sacrament, as shall be well pleasing to thee and profitable to my soul. May your priests continually offer up the Holy Sacrifice in the beauty of holiness, and thy people more and more with devotion and delight throng thine altars. And grant unto thy people that, worthily adoring and receiving thee upon earth, we may all finally by thy mercy be admitted to the heavenly Banquet, where thou, the Lamb which is in the midst of the throne, in unveiled majesty art perfectly worshiped and glorified by countless angels and saints for ever and ever. Amen.

## SPIRITUAL COMMUNION

My Jesus,
I believe that you are present in the Most
    Holy Sacrament.
I love you above all things,
and I desire to receive you into my soul.
Since I cannot at this moment receive you sacramentally,
come at least spiritually into my heart.
I embrace you as if you were already there
and unite myself wholly to you.
Never permit me to be separated from you.
Amen.

---

*Clinton A. Brand, KSG, ed., *St. Gregory's Prayer Book: A Primer of Catholic Devotions from the English Patrimony* (San Francisco: Ignatius Press, 2019), p. 258–259.

## CHAPLET OF THE MOST
## BLESSED SACRAMENT

*Begin with a Spiritual Communion, as above. Then, recalling the 33 years of Our Lord's life, recite 33 times this prayer:*

Jesus, in the Blessed Sacrament, have mercy on us!

## ANIMA CHRISTI

*Anima Christi, sanctifica me.*
*Corpus Christi, salva me.*
*Sanguis Christi, inebria me.*
*Aqua lateris Christi, lava me.*
*Passio Christi, conforta me.*
*O bone Iesu, exaudi me.*
*Intra tua vulnera absconde me.*
*Ne permittas me separari a te.*
*Ab hoste malign defende me.*
*In hora mortis meae voca me.*
*Et iube me venire ad te,*
*ut cum Sanctis tuis laudem te*
*in saecula saeculorum. Amen.*

Soul of Christ, make me holy.
Body of Christ, be my salvation.
Blood of Christ, let me drink your wine.
Water flowing from the side of Christ, wash me clean.
Passion of Christ, strengthen me.
Kind Jesus, hear my prayer.
Hide me within your wound and keep me close to you.
Defend me from the evil enemy
Call me at my death to the fellowship of your saints,
That I may sing your praise with them through all eternity. Amen.

## O SACRAMENT MOST HOLY

O Sacrament most holy,
O Sacrament Divine,
All praise and all thanksgiving
Be every moment Thine.

## *O SACRUM CONVIVIUM* (O SACRED BANQUET)

O sacred Banquet,
wherein Christ is received;
the memory of His Passion is renewed,
the mind is filled with grace,
and the pledge of future glory is given to us.

## A PRAYER OF SAINT THOMAS MORE[*]

Give me the grace to long for your holy sacraments, and
especially to rejoice in the presence of your Body, sweet
Savior Christ, in the holy sacrament of the altar. Amen.

## PRAYER TO OUR LADY OF THE BLESSED SACRAMENT — SAINT JULIAN EYMARD

Virgin Immaculate, perfect lover of Our Lord in the
Blessed Sacrament, we ask you to obtain for us the graces we need to become true adorers of our Eucharistic
God. Grant us, we beg of you, to know Him better, to
love Him more, and to center our lives around the Eucharist, that is, to make our whole life a constant prayer
of adoration, thanksgiving, reparation, and petition to
Our Lord in the Blessed Sacrament. Amen.

V. Pray for us, O Virgin Immaculate, Our Lady of the
Most Blessed Sacrament.
R. That the Eucharistic Kingdom of Jesus Christ may

---

[*] *St. Gregory's Prayer Book*, p. 227

come among us!

## BYZANTINE CATHOLIC PRAYER
## BEFORE HOLY COMMUNION[*]

O Lord, I believe and profess that you are truly Christ, the Son of the living God, who came into the world to save sinners of whom I am the first.

Accept me today as a partaker of your mystical supper, O Son of God, for I will not reveal your mystery to your enemies, nor will I give you a kiss as did Judas, but like the thief I profess you:

Remember me, O Lord, when you come in your
    kingdom.
Remember me, O Master, when you come in your
    kingdom.
Remember me, O Holy One, when you come in your
    kingdom.

May the partaking of your holy mysteries, O Lord, be not for my judgment or condemnation but for the healing of soul and body.

O Lord, I also believe and profess that this, which I am about to receive, is truly your most precious body and your life-giving blood, which, I pray, make me worthy to receive for the remission of all my sins and for life everlasting. Amen.

O God, be merciful to me, a sinner.

---

[*]Divine Liturgies of Our Holy Fathers John Chrysostom and Basil the Great, Byzantine Catholic Metropolitan Church Sui Iuris of Pittsburgh, USA 2006, pp. 77–78.

O God, cleanse me of my sins and have mercy on me.
O Lord, forgive me for I have sinned without number.

## OLD SARUM PRAYER BEFORE COMMUNION†

We beseech thee, O Lord, that this Holy Communion may
be unto us a guide and provision for our journey unto the
haven of everlasting salvation. May it be to us comfort in
sorrow, strength in trial, patience in difficulty, medicine
in sickness, delight in prosperity, and love in all things.
By those most Holy Mysteries which we would receive,
grant us right faith, firm hope, and perfect charity, purification of desire, gladness of mind, ardent love of you, and
a due remembrance of the Passion of your Beloved Son,
with grace to keep our lives full of faith and virtue. And
in the hour of our departure grant that we may receive
this great Mystery with true faith, sure hope, and sincere
charity unto everlasting life. Amen.

## PADRE PIO'S PRAYER AFTER COMMUNION

Stay with me, Lord, because I am weak and I need Your
strength, that I may not fall so often.

Stay with me, Lord, for You are my life, and without
You, I am without meaning and hope.

Stay with me, Lord, for You are my light, and without You, I am in darkness.

Stay with me, Lord, to show me Your will.

Stay with me, Lord, so that I can hear Your voice and
follow you.

Stay with me, Lord, for I desire to love You ever
more, and to be always in Your company.

Stay with me, Lord, if You wish me to be always
faithful to You.

---

†*St. Gregory's Prayer Book*, p. 227

Stay with me, Lord, for as poor as my soul is, I wish it to be a place of consolation for You, a dwelling of Your love.

Stay with me, Jesus, for it is getting late; the days are coming to a close and life is passing. Death, judgement and eternity are drawing near. It is necessary to renew my strength, so that I will not stop along the way, for that I need You. It is getting late and death approaches. I fear the darkness, the temptations, the dryness, the cross, the sorrows. O how I need you, my Jesus, in this night of exile!

Stay with me, Jesus, because in the darkness of life, with all its dangers, I need You.

Help me to recognize You as Your disciples did at the Breaking of the Bread, so that the Eucharist Communion be the light which disperses darkness, the power which sustains me, the unique joy of my heart.

Stay with me, Lord, because at the hour of my death I want to be one with You, and if not by Communion, at least by Your grace and love.

Stay with me, Jesus, I do not ask for divine consolations because I do not deserve them, but I only ask for the gift of Your Presence. Oh yes! I ask this of You.

Stay with me, Lord, for I seek You alone, Your Love, Your Grace, Your Will, Your Heart, Your Spirit, because I love You and I ask for no other reward but to love You more and more, with a strong active love.

Grant that I may love You with all my heart while on earth, so that I can continue to love you perfectly throughout all eternity, dear Jesus.

## PRAYER TAUGHT BY THE GUARDIAN ANGEL OF PORTUGAL TO THE CHILDREN AT FATIMA

Most Holy Trinity, Father, Son, and Holy Spirit, I adore you profoundly. I offer you the most precious Body, Blood, Soul and Divinity of Jesus Christ, present in all the tabernacles of the world, in reparation for the outrages, sacrileges and indifference by which he is offended. And, through the infinite merits of his Most Sacred Heart, and the Immaculate Heart of Mary, I beg of You the conversion of poor sinners.

## PRAYER OF SAINT JOHN HENRY NEWMAN BEFORE ADORATION*

I place myself in the presence of Him, in whose Incarnate Presence I am before I place myself there. I adore You, O my Savior, present here as God and as man, in soul and in body, in true flesh and blood. I acknowledge and confess that I kneel before that Sacred Humanity, which was conceived in Mary's womb, and lay in Mary's bosom; which grew up to twelve, wrought miracles, and spoke words of wisdom and peace; which in due season hung on the cross, lay in the tomb, rose from the dead, and now reigns in heaven. I praise, and bless, and give myself wholly to Him, who is the true Bread of my soul, and my everlasting joy.

## PRAYER OF SAINT ALPHONSUS LIGUORI

My Lord Jesus Christ, who for the love which You bear us, remain night and day in this Sacrament full of compassion and love, awaiting, calling, and welcoming all who come to visit You, I believe that You are present in

*Ibid., 219.

the Sacrament of the Altar. I adore You from the abyss of my nothingness, and I thank You for all the graces which You have bestowed upon me and in particular for having given me Yourself in this Sacrament, for having given me Your most holy Mother Mary as my Advocate, and for having called me to visit You in this church. I now salute Your most loving Heart; and this for three ends: first, in thanksgiving for this great gift; secondly, to make amends to You for all the outrages which You receive in this Sacrament from all Your enemies; thirdly, I intend by this visit to adore You in all the places on earth in which You are present in this Sacrament and in which You are the least reserved and the most abandoned. My Jesus, I love You with all my heart. I grieve for having hitherto so many times offended Your infinite goodness. I purpose by Your grace never more to offend You for the time to come. And now, miserable and unworthy though I be, I consecrate myself to You without reserve; I give You and renounce my entire will, my affections, my desires, and all that I possess. Henceforward, dispose of me and of all that I have as You please. All that I ask of You and desire is Your holy love, final perseverance, and the perfect accomplishment of Your will. I recommend to You the souls in Purgatory, and especially those who had the greatest devotion to the most Blessed Sacrament, and to the most Blessed Virgin Mary. I also recommend to You all poor sinners. Finally, my dear Savior, I unite all my affections with the affections of Your most loving Heart, and I offer them, thus united, to Your Eternal Father, and beseech Him in Your name to vouchsafe for Your love, to accept and grant them.

## PRAYER OF POPE ST. JOHN PAUL II
## FOR A EUCHARISTIC PROCESSION

Lord Jesus, who in the Eucharist make your dwelling among us and become our travelling companion, sustain our Christian communities so that they may be ever more open to listening and accepting your Word. May they draw from the Eucharist a renewed commitment to spreading in society, by the proclamation of your Gospel, the signs and deeds of an attentive and active charity.

Lord Jesus, in your Eucharist make Christian spouses the "signs" of your nuptial love among us: make families communities of people who, living in dialogue with God and each other, do not fear life and become responsible for sowing the seeds of priestly, religious, and missionary vocations.

Lord Jesus, from your altar illuminate this city with light and grace, so that it may reject the seduction of a materialistic conception of life, and defeat the selfishness that threatens it, the injustices that upset it, and the divisions with which it is afflicted.

Lord Jesus: give us your joy, give us your peace.

Stay with us, Lord!

You alone have the words of eternal life!

# IV
# Private
# Meditation

# 11

# Eucharistic Reflections on the Four Purposes of Prayer

*By Fr. Jeffrey Kirby, STL*

When we spend time with Our Lord in the Blessed Sacrament, we can focus our minds and hearts through the four purposes or forms of prayer, sometimes summarized with the acronym ACTS: Adoration, Contrition, Thanksgiving, Supplication. The following reflections are meant to draw us deeper into each form of prayer; read them slowly and thoughtfully, or use them as a starting point for your own conversation with Jesus.

## ADORATION

As we approach our Eucharistic Lord, let our hearts be filled with adoration. We see the Lord of glory and majesty come to us. He is all-holy. He is the sovereign of all. And yet, he comes to us and is present to us under the form of a small piece of bread. We acknowledge his presence. We praise his greatness. We exalt in his splendor. We give homage to his power, which frees us from sin and evil and allows us to worship him without fear. We praise him!

As we adore our Eucharistic Lord, we consider the wonders of his greatness. We announce in our hearts the magnificence of our God, as we allow our hearts to leap and dance for joy. We acknowledge the illustriousness of his goodness. We exalt in the sublimity of his kindness. We know how much he loves us! Who are we to merit such love, such benevolence, from so glorious a king? And yet, he comes to us now. He is present before us. There is the all-holy God, humble and present to us under the form of bread.

We exclaim with the angels, "Holy, holy, holy is the LORD of hosts! / All the earth is filled with his glory" (Is 6:3), and continue with the prophet Isaiah: "Woe is me, I am doomed! For I am a man of unclean lips, living among a people of unclean lips; and my eyes have seen the King, the LORD of hosts!" (Is 6:5).

Yes, the Lord of hosts comes to us! He is there! Before us right now! List the attributes of the King. Shed the sorrows of life. Move above the melancholy of a fallen world. The King, the Ancient of Days, and the All-Glorious One is here. Praise him!

## CONTRITION

As we approach our Eucharistic Lord, let our hearts be filled with contrition. We see the Perfect and All-Holy One, who is also the Most Compassionate and All-Loving One, before us. He comes to us, not as a judge now, but as Savior and Companion. He desires to be with us and walk with us through life.

The Lord comes to us and is present to us under the form of a small piece of bread. As we see his divine humility, we are moved to repentance. We confess our own unworthiness to be with him, to receive such companionship, and to be so greatly loved. And yet, the Lord truly loves us. He desires to walk with us. He does everything possible to show us his love and mercy. He comes to us under the form of bread.

As we repent before the Eucharistic Lord, we examine our consciences and confess our sins. Let us declare how much we detest anything that takes us away from the Lord's presence or diminishes our love for him. We welcome you, Lord! We seek to follow you! We confess and denounce our sins! We resolve never to sin again! We desire to live always in your love and to rejoice always in your presence!

We exclaim with King David: "Have mercy on me, God, in accord with your steadfast love; / in your abundant compassion blot out my transgressions. / Thoroughly wash away my guilt; / and from my sin cleanse me" (Ps 51:1–2).

Yes, the King of Mercy comes to us! He is before us — there in the Blessed Sacrament! Confess your sins. Dispel the darkness. Draw close to the Eucharistic Lord who loves you and forgives you. The Good Shepherd, the Ocean of Mercy, the Font of Goodness, is here. Trust him!

## THANKSGIVING

As we approach our Eucharistic Lord, let our hearts be filled with thanksgiving. The Source of Goodness and the Giver of every good gift comes to us. He is extraordinary in his kindness and overwhelming in his generosity! He is the Alpha and the Omega, the beginning and end of all things! And yet, he comes to us and is present to us under the form of a small piece of bread. We exalt in his presence. We are humbled by his goodness. We explode in our gratitude and abound in thanksgiving to him! We praise you, and we thank you, Lord!

As we give thanks to our Eucharistic Lord, we consider his many blessings and acts of kindness to us, from the general blessings given to all, to the particular blessings given just to us; from the blessings we have asked for, to the blessings that he has freely given to us. We glorify him! We rejoice! We express all the gratitude of our hearts, thanking him and praising him with our whole being.

We exclaim with King David: "Give thanks to the LORD, invoke his name; / make known among the peoples his deeds. / Sing praise, play music, / proclaim all his wonderful deeds" (1 Chr 16:8–9).

Yes, the Lord of Glory comes to us! All good gifts come from him. He is the source of all kindness. He comes to us. He is there in the monstrance before us! He is with us. Acclaim his goodness and list his blessings in your heart. Declare his acts of kindness to you. Exalt in his benevolence. Rejoice! The Friend of Sinners, the Mighty God, the Prince of Peace, is here. Give him thanks!

## SUPPLICATION

As we approach our Eucharistic Lord, let our hearts be filled with supplication. The Good Shepherd is here. He is meek and humble of heart. He is loving and compassionate toward those in need. He is the All-Powerful and Ever-Living God, and yet he comes to us and is present to us under the form of a small piece of bread. He is Love. He is Mercy. He wishes to walk with us and to hear our needs.

As we offer our supplications to the Eucharistic Lord, we can hear him ask us what perplexes us, worries us, or scares us. As we hear the Lord's question, and see his presence in the Eucharist before us, we can trust him and open our hearts to him. We can speak candidly to him, sincerely disclosing our concerns, needs, and heartaches to him. We trust you, Lord; we rely on your goodness to us.

We exclaim with Saint Paul: "Have no anxiety at all, but in everything, by prayer and petition, with thanksgiving, make your requests known to God. Then the peace of God that surpasses all understanding will guard your hearts and minds in Christ Jesus" (Phil 4:6–7).

Yes, the Lord, our provider, comes to us. The Lord, our peace, is here. We are beggars before him, but he makes us the children of God. We ask for bread, and he blesses us. We ask for fish, and he provides for us. The Lord is with us! He is overflowing in kindness. Open your heart and offer your petitions. Declare your trust in him. Exalt in his goodness! The God who sees, the song and strength of his people, is here. Offer him your supplications!

# 12
# A Brief Guide to *Lectio Divina*

*Lectio divina*, or "divine reading," is an ancient method of praying with the scriptures and a beautiful way of kindling our love and devotion to our Lord in the Blessed Sacrament.

Begin by placing yourself in the presence of God, who is present on the altar, and tell him you want to enter into a conversation with him.

## STEP 1: READ THE PASSAGE
Select a passage from scripture, whether one of those suggested below, the readings of the liturgical day, or any verses that appeal to you. Read the text through, opening your heart to the words but not worrying about what they mean or what you might think you're "supposed to" get out of the passage. If you want, read the passage through a couple of times. See below for some eucharistic selections.

## STEP 2: MEDITATE
Spend a few minutes pondering the passage. Relate to it from your life or your day. Think about what the words mean and consider where the text may be challenging you or showing you something new. This is a good time to write out your thoughts.

## STEP 3: PRAY
Now, bring your meditation to God and begin a conversation with him. You might ask him what he wants to tell you through these words, give him the fears or challenges you discovered, or just talk to him about what struck you while you were medi-

tating. If you have trouble focusing, write out your half of the conversation.

## STEP 4: CONTEMPLATE

Contemplation is the real heart of *lectio*. Open your heart to the Holy Spirit, asking him to stir up in you a deep love of God. Sit silently, knowing God's love for you and returning love to him. True contemplation is a gift of the Holy Spirit; don't worry if you don't feel like you've achieved great spiritual heights in today's prayer. Just love God and let him work in your heart.

## SUGGESTED SCRIPTURE PASSAGES

Matthew 15:29–37
Matthew 19:16–22
Mark 14:12–16, 22–26
Mark 15:16–20
Luke 9:11b–17
Luke 22:39–44
Luke 24:13–35
John 6:1–15
John 6:24–35
John 6:41–51
John 6:51–58
John 19:31–37
John 21:1–14

# CONTRIBUTORS

## BISHOP KEVIN C. RHOADES

After leading the Diocese of Harrisburg, Pennsylvania, for five years, Bishop Kevin C. Rhoades was appointed to the Diocese of Fort Wayne-South Bend, Indiana, and installed there as bishop in January 2010. Bishop Rhoades currently serves as a member of the U.S. Conference of Catholic Bishops' Committee on Doctrine and the USCCB Committee on Religious Liberty, of which he is chair-elect, assuming the chair in November 2023. He is presently vice chair of the board of trustees of Mount St. Mary's Seminary and is chair of the board of directors of Our Sunday Visitor. Ordained to the priesthood in 1983, Bishop Rhoades received his license degrees (STL) in sacred theology and in canon law (JCL) from the Pontifical Gregorian University in Rome.

## FR. JEFFREY KIRBY, STD

**Fr. Jeffrey Kirby, STD,** is the pastor of Our Lady of Grace Parish in Indian Land, South Carolina. He is a moral theologian and Papal Missionary of Mercy. He serves as adjunct professor of theology at Belmont Abbey College and is the author of several books, including *Understanding the Bible: A Catholic Guide to Applying God's Word to Your Life Today* (OSV, 2022).